C000216047

THE CRY OF MY HEART

One thing that really matters – is to be **genuine**... to be **authentic.**

So what does it mean to be a **genuine disciple?** These studies explore Jesus' blueprint for life from **The Sermon on the Mount** so that you can learn to follow Jesus His way...

7 BIBLE STUDIES FOR SMALL GROUPS

BY TIM HAWKINS

The Cry of my Heart: Bible Study Book

This UK edition © 2007 Tim Hawkins/The Good Book Company

This edition published in the UK by The Good Book Company
Elm House, 37 Elm Road
New Malden, Surrey KT3 3HB, UK
Phone: 0845 225 0880
E-mail: admin@thegoodbook.co.uk
Website: www.thegoodbook.co.uk

Published in Australia by Hawkins Ministry Resources
42 York Road, Kellyville. NSW 2155 Australia
Phone/Fax: (+61 2) 9629 6569
E-mail: info@hawkinsministry.com
Website: www.hawkinsministry.com

All Scripture quotations, unless otherwise indicated, are taken from The Holy Bible:
New International Version. © 1973, 1978, 1984 by International Bible Society.
Used by permission of Zondervan Publishing House. All rights reserved.

ISBN: 9781905564798

All rights reserved. No part of this publication may be reproduced, stored in a retrieval system, or
transmitted in any form or by any means – electronic, mechanical, photocopy, recording, or any other –
except for brief quotations in printed reviews, without the prior permission of the publisher.

Printed in the UK

CONTENTS

GENUINE SUCCESS

Matthew 5:1-12

1. MY VIEW OF SUCCESS

In the space below, draw a picture of a person – or a group of people – that you think are "successful". You might draw some sports players, or musicians, or business people... draw anyone you like! Include in your drawing the things that these people have achieved that makes them successful.

'JESUS WANTS TO GIVE YOU THE GAME PLAN FOR YOUR LIFE'

2. JESUS' VIEW OF SUCCESS

Read Matthew 5:1-12, and fill in the chart below by identifying the eight pictures that Jesus gives of the person who is truly "blessed" or "successful".

Verse	"Blessed are..."	"... for ..."	How could this describe me in my own life?
3			
4			
5			
6			
7			
8			
9			
10-12			

3. MY DISCIPLESHIP

Look back over Jesus' eight pictures of a genuine disciple on the previous page, and fill in the chart below:

The discipleship picture where I feel I am the strongest is:	
This is how I can use this "strength" to help others:	
The discipleship picture where I feel I am the weakest is:	
This is what I can do to grow stronger in this area of weakness:	

ARE YOU ACHIEVING WHAT IS REALLY WORTH ACHIEVING?

4. WHEN THE GOING GETS TOUGH...

Read again Jesus' words in **Matthew 5:10-11**.

a) Think of a situation where other people were making it hard for you to stand up as a Christian. What did they do? What did you do?

b) How can a Christian group support you, so you are better able to keep going for Jesus when times are tough?

c) Pray for each other in your group. Use the answers that people have shared as a basis for praying for each person individually.

FOR MORE INFO:

Read Chapters 1-4 in
The Cry of my Heart

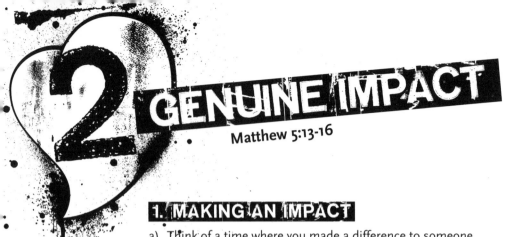

2 GENUINE IMPACT
Matthew 5:13-16

1. MAKING AN IMPACT

a) Think of a time where you made a difference to someone else's life. What happened? What did you do? What was the result?

b) Think of a time where **as a Christian** you tried to make a difference to someone else's **spiritual** life. What happened? What did you do? What was the result?

2. SALT AND LIGHT

Read Matthew 5: 13-16 and fill in the chart below.

a) Think of the different things that "salt" can do. Write down as many different uses as you can.	b) How can you live your life so that you will be like "salt" to those around you?
c) Think of the different things that "light" can do. Write down as many different uses as you can.	d) How can you live your life so that you will be like "light" to those around you?

e) According to Jesus, how can salt lose its effectiveness?

f) According to Jesus, how can light lose its effectiveness?

g) What warning does this give us as Christians?

3. THE LIGHT OF THE WORLD

Read again Matthew 5:14-16.
Jesus says we are the "light of the world". But the Bible also talks about **God** being like "light". How do these verses help us understand our role as "light" in this world?

a)   Psalm 36:9

b)   Psalm 18:28

c)   Psalm 19:8

d)   Psalm 76:4

e)   Psalm 119:105

f)   John 1:4-5

g)   John 1:9

h)   John 3:19-21

i)   John 8:12

j)   John 12:35-36

k)   1 Peter 2:9

l)   1 John 1:5-7

m)   1 John 2:9

n)   Revelation 22:5

o) **Read Ephesians 5:8-14**

How does Ephesians 5:8-14 help you understand what it means to be "light"?

4. PUTTING IT ALL TOGETHER

a) Here is what "hit" me the most in this study about my own life as a disciple:

b) Here is what "hit" me the most in this study about how I need to relate to my non-christian friends:

c) Pray for each other – that we will be "salt" and "light" to our non-Christian friends, who need to discover Jesus.

FOR MORE INFO:

Read Chapters 5-6 in
The Cry of my Heart

3 GENUINE OBEDIENCE
Matthew 5:17-48

1. WHY ARE THERE SO MANY RULES?

Finish the chart below by writing down some of the rules that you are expected to obey.

	Here are some rules that I don't **mind** obeying	Here are some rules that I don't **like** obeying
At home		
At school / work		
At church / youth group / camp		
God's rules		

Look at each of Jesus' six examples. As well as writing down the original command, try and work out how people **might** have got it wrong. Then show Jesus' true meaning!

Verse	"You have heard it said"	"This doesn't mean..."	"The real meaning"	"Go even further"
21-26				
27-30				
31-32				
33-37				
38-42				
43-47				

3. MY OWN EXAMPLES

Think of your own example of a command that God gives in the Bible. Then show the right way to approach that law. What might be some of the steps that you would need to avoid because they might take you towards that sin?

A command that God has given to prevent us from sinning	Here are some of the steps I must avoid because they will take me closer to that sin

YOU USUALLY START ON THE PATH BY THINKING ABOUT THE SIN, IMAGINING WHAT IT WOULD BE LIKE, AND THEN PLANNING TO DO IT!

4. MY OWN DISCIPLESHIP

Can you see it's possible to **look** like you're obeying God, when deep down you're not trusting Him at all?

a) Here is an example of where I sometimes end up obeying God without really trusting Him:

b) As a result of what I've learned today, here is an area of my discipleship where I'm going to start obeying God in a whole new way:

c) Pray for each other – that our obedience will always be genuine!

FOR MORE INFO:

Read Chapters 7-10 in
The Cry of my Heart

'JESUS HAS WON THE BATTLE, AND WE ARE ON THE VICTORY LAP'

4 GENUINE WORSHIP

Matthew 6:1-18

1. WHY I DO CHRISTIAN THINGS

In each column, tick the main reasons why you are involved these Christian activities. You may have as many ticks in eac column as you like – but be as honest as you can.

	Why I go to church	Why I go to youth group	Why I came today
All my friends go			
For all the great activities			
I want to grow as a Christian			
My parents make me go			
It's a cheap night out			
My girlfriend/boyfriend goes			
I get along well the leaders			
I want to please my parents			
I like learning more about God			
I enjoy the fellowship of other Christians			
There are lots of girls/guys to meet			
Anything to get away from home!			
It's the only thing my parents let me go to			
I want to become a Christian			
I've gone all my life			
I want my friends to find out about Jesus			
Everyone expects me to go			
I like hassling the leaders			
I'd feel guilty if I missed			
I want to encourage the others			
I want to support my church			
(write your own!)			

2. JESUS' WARNINGS

Jesus warns us about doing the right thing for the wrong reason!
Check out these four examples:

Activity	The error to avoid	The right way
When being generous **6:2-4**		
When praying **6:5-6**		
6:7-15		
When fasting **6:16-18**		

3. DANGEROUS WORSHIP

Look through each of these passages. See if they help you to understand what it really means to follow God with genuine worship.

• *What is wrong with the spiritual life of these people?*
• *How do you think God feels about this?*
• *How does this passage help me in my own discipleship and worship?*

a) Amos 5:18-24

b) Malachi 1:8-14

c) Revelation 3:14-16

4. MY OWN DISCIPLESHIP

a) Here is a Christian activity that sometimes I end up doing for the wrong reason:

b) Here is one thing I have learned from today's study that will help me to live my life as a genuine disciple:

c) Pray for each other – and praise God with genuine worship!

FOR MORE INFO:
Read Chapters 11-14 in
The Cry of my Heart

5 GENUINE TRUST

Matthew 6:19-34

1. WHAT I REALLY WANT

In the space below, draw a picture or write a list of all the things you would love to own if you had unlimited money. The sky's the limit! What would you really like?

"WHAT'S REALLY IMPORTANT TO YOU?"

2. MY HEART AND MY RICHES

Read Matthew 6:19-24

a) What is the problem with trusting in "riches on earth"? **(verse 19)**

b) What examples can you think of where you've got something "new", but the glamour of it fades away pretty quickly?

c) What do you think Jesus means by "riches in heaven"? **(verse 20)**
   What are some of the riches that you are storing up there?

d) What effect do your "treasures" (what's important to you) have on your "heart" (the very centre of your life)? **(verse 21).**
   How can this be a real trap for a Christian?

e) Why can't you have both? Why can't you devote your life to everything that non-Christians do **AND** devote it to God as well? **(verse 24)**

f) Right now – what are the things that are dominating your thinking in your life?
   What does this tell you about where your heart is?

Tick the things that you sometimes worry about. Tick as many as apply!

- ❏ whether everything will be okay at home
- ❏ will I be able to get a job that I like?
- ❏ nuclear threat – terrorism – global warming – is there any future for us?
- ❏ if I don't join in what my friends do, then they mightn't like me
- ❏ I'm not as tall / thin / attractive / strong as my friends
- ❏ I don't seem to have many good friends
- ❏ I often seem to fail
- ❏ being unemployed
- ❏ pimples
- ❏ getting overweight
- ❏ my mum and dad are splitting up
- ❏ I want to be accepted like all my friends
- ❏ whether my parents will be proud of me
- ❏ whether I'll get invited to the next party or big event
- ❏ not having enough money for the things I want
- ❏ my friends at school might find out I'm a Christian
- ❏ people who do the wrong thing seem to get away with it
- ❏ if people knew what I was really like, they mightn't accept me
- ❏ no one seems to have problems like me
- ❏ letting my parents down
- ❏ when people get angry at me
- ❏ when mum and dad fight
- ❏ feeling alone
- ❏ people who hurt me
- ❏ going bald
- ❏ I'm not sure if God will accept me
- ❏ not having a boyfriend / girlfriend
- ❏ when people treat me like a "kid"
- ❏ when I get caught for something I've done wrong
- ❏ will I do okay in my exams this year?
- ❏ when I'm involved in things I know are wrong, and I can't seem to stop
- ❏ I'm not sure whether I'll make it to heaven
- ❏ no one seems to understand me
- ❏ will my parents give me the freedom I want?
- ❏ I don't think I'm good enough to be a Christian
- ❏ ....
- ❏ ....

> *Now pick the "top three" things that you tend to worry about, and write them down here:*
>
> 1.
>
> 2.
>
> 3.

4. PUT GOD'S KINGDOM FIRST

Read Matthew 6:25-34

a) Jesus tells two stories to show why there is no real need to worry. What are these two stories?

    i. 6:26

    ii. 6:28-30

'SEEK FIRST GOD'S KINGDOM' — THAT'S THE CRY OF MY HEART!'

b) What reasons does Jesus give you so you won't worry too much about problems in your life?

i, 6:27

ii. 6:31-32

c) **Read Matthew 6:33 again**
    i. Rewrite 6:33 as a motto for your life.

    ii. If you really concentrate on God, and what He's done for you, what will happen to all the other things that you really need?

    iii Pray to God with prayers of trust. Tell Him what you're prepared to give up so that nothing will get in the way of following Him.

FOR MORE INFO:

Read Chapters 15-18 in
The Cry of my Heart

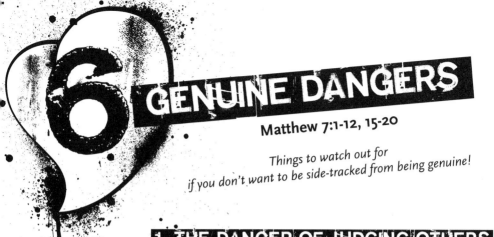

6 GENUINE DANGERS

Matthew 7:1-12, 15-20

*Things to watch out for
if you don't want to be side-tracked from being genuine!*

1. THE DANGER OF JUDGING OTHERS

a) What are some of the things that other people do in your everyday life that you find **so annoying?**

b) What are some of the things that other people do at your church, or in your Christian group that you find **so annoying?**

Read Matthew 7:1-6

c) What reasons does Jesus give for not judging others?

d) What is the correct way to treat others? How will this help you to be genuine as a disciple?

e) Jot down one area of your life where you can take this warning seriously.

2. THE DANGER OF NOT TRUSTING GOD

Read Matthew 7:7-12

a) What do these verses tell you about what God is like?

b) What does God want you to do about the issues in your life?

c) What will be the result of trusting God in prayer?

d) Rewrite 7:12 in your own words, so it can be a motto for your life.

e) What are some of the things that God wants you to trust Him for – right now?

"NO MATTER WHAT IT FEELS LIKE, GOD WILL NEVER LET US DOWN"

3. THE DANGER OF LISTENING TO THE WRONG PEOPLE

Read Matthew 7:15-20

a) What test does Jesus give us so that we can know whether someone is teaching us the truth from the Bible? **(verses 16 and 20)**

b) What is the fate of anyone who does not bear "good fruit"?

c) How do these warnings help you stay on the right track as a Christian?

d) Finish this statement:
"If the devil were trying to tempt me to be a little less obedient to Jesus today, here is the area where he's most likely to have some success:"

e) Finish by praying as a group. "Ask, seek and knock" as you bring every request before your God. Pray for each other, that you might remain genuine and not be side-tracked by these dangers.

FOR MORE INFO:

Read Chapters 19, 20, 22 in
The Cry of my Heart

7 GENUINE COMMITMENT

Matthew 7:13-14, 21-29

1. ARE MY WORDS GENUINE?

Read Matthew 7:21-23

a) How does Jesus distinguish between those who just "say" they are following Him, and those who are truly genuine?
What do you think He means by this?

b) Focus on the words that Jesus will say to those who **claim** to have followed Him, but were not truly genuine. **(verse 23)** How do you think it would feel to have Jesus say those words to you on Judgment Day?

c) What do you think Jesus **will** say to you when you finally do stand before Him to be judged?

d) Check out what Jesus **does** say to those who do genuinely follow Him in **Matthew 25:23 and Matthew 25:34.** How do you know what words you **will** hear from Jesus?

"IF YOU DON'T STAND FOR SOMETHING,
YOU'LL FALL FOR ANYTHING"

2. IS MY LIFE GENUINE?

Read Matthew 7:24-29

a) What does Jesus say is the real difference between these two house-builders?

b) Which one best describes how you're living as a Christian right now?

c) What changes do you think Jesus wants you to make to your life right now?

Read Matthew 7:13-14 and study the digram below which represents the two roads that Jesus is talking about.

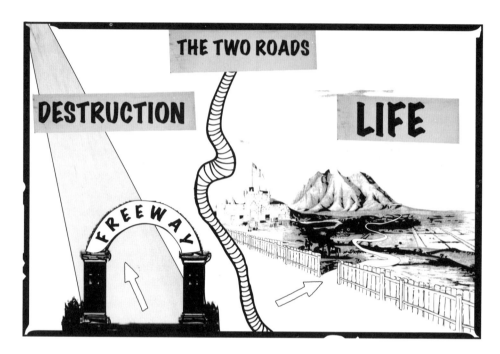

Think carefully about where you are up to in your spiritual journey, and mark the diagram with an "X" to show where **you** stand in relation to Jesus. Have you just started to follow Jesus – or are you a long way down the track in being His disciple? Have you realised that you're really living without Him – and you need to place yourself on the other road? Or are you just at the start trying to make your mind up?

*Write out your own
prayer of commitment.*

*Say to Jesus
whatever is on your heart.*

*Pray together with
the rest of your group.*

*Pray that each one of you
will be genuine in your
commitment so that you keep
on enjoying Jesus for eternity.*

FOR MORE INFO:

Read Chapters 21, 23, 24 in
The Cry of my Heart

OVERTIME CHALLENGE
THE BIG QUESTION

HOW DO I KNOW IF I'M REALLY A CHRISTIAN?

God's Answer:

- Ephesians 1:4
- John 6:37, 39, 44, 65
- John 10:27-29
- Romans 8:35-39
- 2 Timothy 4:18
- Philippians 1:6
- Ephesians 1:13-14
- Jude 24-25
- 1 John 5:11-13
- Romans 10:9
- John 3:16

Three questions to help you sort it out:
(answer each question with "Yes", "No" or "I don't know")

1. Have you genuinely asked Jesus to forgive all your sins and take your punishment by His death on the cross?

2. Have you genuinely asked Jesus to take your life over and start running it His way?

3. Do you now want to live the rest of your life obeying Jesus – no matter what it might cost you?

SO HOW DO I KNOW IF I'M GENUINE – OR JUST A VERY GOOD COUNTERFEIT?
(check upside-down answer!)

Do you want to be genuine? Tell Jesus!

29

LEADER'S NOTES

THE SERIES

The aim of the whole series is to help students to become genuine disciples. To do this, these studies follow Jesus' blueprint for life contained in the Sermon on the Mount, in Matthew Chs 5-7.

a) For each study...
There is more material in some studies than you will need for your group. You need to select precisely what you will do as you encourage your students to become genuine disciples. It's okay to leave some sections out! But please work through all the material yourself. You need to know it all – even if some of it is only background material. The aim of each study is that your students will **put it into action**. You do not necessarily need to finish every single question. Use as much of this material as your group needs to put into action in their own life how God is growing them to be genuine. Finally, make your small group a powerhouse of prayer. Make prayer central, not an "add-on" extra.

b) Take time to grow your group
Take the time to help people in your group get to know each other, feel comfortable about sharing, and start to build a mini-community. If your group is new – where the students don't necessarily know each other – you may want to start with some introductory games or activities. You work out what will suit your group the best. Here are some suggestions:

- *Have each person introduce themselves, their school, their favourite food / movie.*
- *Have each person write down the answers to 5 questions (favourite things etc.) and then mix them up and have everyone guess who wrote which set of answers.*
- *Divide into 2 and have each person introduce their partner.*

c) Extra Resources
"The Cry Of My Heart" – The Book! This easy-to-read book is designed with teenagers in mind, and contains great background material for each study. This study booklet follows a similar sequence to the original book – so it's easy to follow along. Make sure you are reading the book yourself ahead of each week's study. Perhaps you could make a book available for each of your group? If you are using the book, note the following variations from these studies:

- **Section 1 in the book** *Genuine Success* is divided into two separate studies (*Genuine Success* and *Genuine Impact*) to give more emphasis to being salt and light. Therefore the numbering of the following studies will always be one different from the book.
- **Studies 6 and 7** (*Genuine Dangers* and *Genuine Commitment*) are divided differently from the book to more evenly divide the material in Matthew 7.

STUDY 1 – GENUINE SUCCESS

The aim of this study: To contrast what the world sees as "success" with what Jesus sees as "success" so that your group can become **genuine disciples.** Each of Jesus' eight pictures of a genuine disciple start with the world "blessed" – that is, this person is to be congratulated! This person has achieved what is worth achieving! This person is becoming the success that Jesus wants.

In Question 2: The first 2 columns are analysing Jesus' words – but the 3rd column is for application. Can your group turn each of Jesus' pictures into an attitude that they should have? Here are some ideas to get you started:
v 3: "I know I really need God"
v 4: "I'm upset by the sin I see"
v 5: "I don't force my own way"
v 6: "I want things done God's way"
v 7: "I want to treat people like Jesus treats me"
v 8: "I'm not pretending to be Christian"
v 9: "I want to forgive and accept others"
v 10: "I'm prepared to be rejected because I follow Jesus"

In Questions 3-4: Take note of each member's strengths and weaknesses so that you might follow them up appropriately.

STUDY 2 – GENUINE IMPACT

The aim of this study: To help your group see that their power to change the lives of those around them lies in the fact that they are **different.**

They have a different set of values. They have a different set of beliefs. They have a different style of behaviour. This is the essential nature of both "salt" and "light". Both of them change their environment because they are **essentially different** from the things that they penetrate. Salt only loses its effectiveness when it is no longer salty. Light only loses its effectiveness when it is covered up. **(Question 2)**

Question 3: Choose ahead of time which of these verses will be most appropriate for your group.

STUDY 3 – GENUINE OBEDIENCE

The aim of this study: To show your group that genuine obedience isn't just complying outwardly (and maybe even resenting it at the same time!). It's not doing the bare minimum and seeing how much you can get away with. Jesus' approach to obedience is: If something is a sin against God, **then don't even take the first step on the path that might lead you there!**

Question 2: In this chart, where you analyse the six commandments that Jesus uses as illustrations, note that Column 2 ("This doesn't mean") requires you to interpret what the **wrong** understanding of that law might be. You will not find this answer in the text, but it will help you to understand the right answer!

Question 3: Try and think of some of God's laws that your group might particularly struggle with – and work out the wrong and right ways of understanding these commandments.

Question 4: Help your group to understand the contrast between these two attitudes. Only one of them is genuine obedience!

STUDY 4 – GENUINE WORSHIP

The aim of this study: This study continues the theme of Study 3 – that it is entirely possible to do **right** things for the **wrong** reasons. The three examples that Jesus gives (*generosity, prayer* and *fasting*) show that if you're doing these things to seek your own reward – then that's the only reward you're going to get!

You may get some questions about **fasting**. Very briefly, people often abstained from food to help them focus on their prayers (the two are usually linked in Scripture). It is a way of denying yourself so that you can acknowledge your dependence on God. Group members probably should not fast without first consulting their parents!

Question 1: If you're doing these studies as part of a camp, use Column 3 so that the group can answer "Why I came on this camp".

STUDY 5 – GENUINE TRUST

The aim of this study: To challenge what we really trust in. To show that God can be trusted to deal with the things that we so often "worry" about. Putting God first in our lives means that everything else can fit into the right place.

Questions 1-2: These show that one sure way to check our heart – is to check what we're putting our money into. This could come up with some telling answers for your group!

Questions 3-4: You may need to point out that while Jesus tells us not to "worry" about things, that doesn't mean we shouldn't be "concerned" about them. *Eg: If we're feeling sick, a wrong approach would be to worry and worry about it in a way that showed we didn't trust God. But it would be equally wrong to show no concern at all (eg: not seek medical help but keep putting yourself in him).* What Jesus is talking about here is – can we trust God enough to let **Him** do the worrying for us? Because if we **don't** trust Him, then we'll need to do all the worrying about it ourselves. According to **Matthew 7:7-11**, the alternative to unhelpful worry – is prayer!

Matthew 6:33 is a key verse. Spend some time, not only "rewriting" it, but also working through what it means for each person.

STUDY 6 – GENUINE DANGERS

The aim of this study: To show that there are dangers surrounding us that will attempt to side-track us from being genuine disciples.

Question 1: This shows the danger of using Jesus'

teaching as ammunition to criticise someone else! One mark of a true disciple is that they deal with the plank in their own eye before being critical of the specks in others!

Question 2: Shows the danger of not coming to God in prayer because we're scared He'll say "no". One mark of a genuine disciple is that they commit everything to God in prayer.

Question 3: This shows the danger of listening to false teaching. While this can be hard for a young disciple to discern, and they may need wisdom and guidance from those more experienced in the faith, the key point that Jesus gives us about false teachers is *"by their fruit you shall know them"*.

STUDY 7 – GENUINE COMMITMENT

The aim of this study: This study aims to help the group check whether their commitment to Jesus is genuine.

Question 1: This helps the group to make sure they're not just getting the **actions** right – without an inward change of heart that treats Jesus as Lord.

These words from Jesus are very blunt. For the person who is only pretending, these words should be a wake-up call to be genuine in following Jesus. But to the committed (but perhaps insecure) Christian, these words might cause unnecessary worry. Make sure you contrast them with the words that Jesus speaks in Question 1d.

The question (1 d) *"How do you know what words Jesus will speak to you?"* is a very important one. The answer depends on two things:
- The certainty of what Jesus has done for me in His death and resurrection.
- The genuineness of the response that I am making to Him.
Some of the verses in the *Overtime Challenge* might be helpful here.

Question 2: This helps members make sure they're not just hearing God without responding to Him.

Question 3: This helps the group clarify what their **actual commitment** to Jesus really means.

Even though this passage comes earlier than the others, it has been left to last deliberately so that the group will have the maximum amount of information before completing this question.

Where your members place themselves in this picture is of vital importance. Encourage them to be honest in what they say. Use the information they give you to guide your follow-up with them.

OVERTIME CHALLENGE

This is an "extra" to help those who might come up with this perplexing question:
"I know what it means for someone to be a Christian – but how do I know whether my response is genuine or not?"

The Bible verses: This is an assortment of verses which speak the most clearly on this issue. Read them through ahead of time so that you can direct your group to the most appropriate ones for their situation.

The three questions: By answering *"yes"*, *"no"* or *"not sure"* to each question, members can work out whether they really are genuine in following Jesus.
- Question 1 – helps work out whether they really are treating Jesus as **Saviour.**
- Question 2 – helps work out whether they really are treating Jesus as **Lord.**
- Question 3 – helps work out whether they are genuine about **repenting.**

How to interpret the answers:
- 3 *"yes"* answers – most likely this person is a genuine disciple.
- 3 *"no"* or *"not sure"* answers – most likely this person is **not** a genuine disciple (and probably not ready to become one either).
- *"No"* or *"not sure"* to the first 2 questions, with a *"yes"* to the 3rd question – most likely this person is **not yet** a genuine disciple – **but they're now ready to become one!**

So how do I know if I'm really genuine?
The answer might seem simplistic – *"Do you want to be genuine?"* – but if the answer is *"yes"* – then the challenge for that person is to never let the day come when they no longer want to be genuine!
"He who stands firm to the end will be saved." – **Matthew 24:13.**